Christmas Carols for Melodica

Christmas Carols for Melodica

Easy Songs!

Christmas Carols for Melodica: Easy Songs!
© 2012 by Javier Marcó

ISBN-13:978-1481004428
ISBN-10:1481004425

This Christmas I've got a lot of gifts for you!

and also...

We're going to play and sing christmas carols together!

Contents

Playing guide

Standard notation
Notes are written on a Staff.

Staff
The staff consists of five lines and four spaces, on which notes symbols are placed.

Clef
A clef assigns an individual note to a certain line.
The **Treble Clef** or **G Clef** is used for the Melodica.

This clef indicates the position of the note G which is on the second line from the bottom.

Note
A note is a sign used to represent the relative pitch of a sound. There are seven notes:
A, B, C, D, E, F and G.

A   B   C   D   E   F   G

Ledger lines
The ledger lines are used to inscribe notes outside the lines and spaces of the staff.

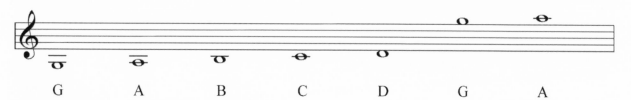

G   A   B   C   D   G   A

Accidentals
An accidental is a symbol to raise or lower the pitch of a note.

♯ sharp   Next note up half step.

♭ flat   Next note down half step.

♮ natural   Cancels a flat or a sharp.

Note values

A **note value** is used to indicate the duration of a note. A **rest** is an interval of silence, marked by a sign indicating the length of the pause. Each rest corresponds to a particular note value.

○	Whole note	▬	Whole rest
𝅗𝅥	Half note	▬	Half rest
𝅘𝅥	Quarter note	𝄽	Quarter rest
𝅘𝅥𝅮	Eight note	𝄾	Eight rest
𝅘𝅥𝅯	Sixteenth note	𝄿	Sixteenth rest

Dotted note

A dotted note is a note with a small dot written after it. The dot adds half as much again to the basic note's duration.

Tie

A tie is a curved line connecting the heads of two notes of the same pitch, indicating that they are to be played as a single note with a duration equal to the sum of the individual notes' note values.

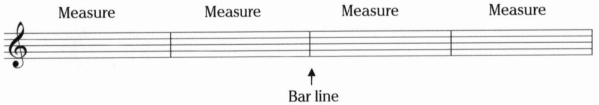

Bars or Measures

The staff is divided into equal segments of time consisting of the same number of beats, called bar or measures.

Measure   Measure   Measure   Measure

↑
Bar line

Time signature

Time signature consists of two numbers, the upper number specifies how many beats (or counts) are in each measure, and the lower number tells us the note value which represents one beat.

one   two   three   four

Example: 4/4 means four quarters, or four beats per measure with a quarter note receiving one beat or count.

Key signature

A Key signature is a group of accidentals, generally written at the beginning of a score immediately after the clef, and shows which notes always get sharps or flats. Accidentals on the lines and spaces in the key signature affect those notes throughout the piece unless there is a natural sign.

Repeat sign

The repeat sign indicates a section should be repeated from the beginning, and then continue on. A corresponding sign facing the other way indicates where the repeat is to begin.

Repeat Sign

First and second endings

The section should be repeated from the beginning, and number brackets above the bars indicate which to played the first time (1), which to play the second time (2).

Fingering

In this book right hand fingering is indicated using numbers above the staff, and left hand fingering is indicated using numbers below the staff.

1= thumb
2= index
3= middle
4= ring
5= little finger

Dynamics

Dynamics refers to the volume of the notes.

p   (piano), meaning soft.
mp   (mezzo-piano), meaning "moderately soft".
mf   (mezzo-forte), meaning "moderately loud".
f   (forte), meaning loud.

Crescendo. A gradual increase in volume.

Decrescendo. A gradual decrease in volume.

Tempo Markings

Tempo is written at the beginning of a piece of music and indicates how slow or fast this piece should be played.

Lento — very slow (40–60 bpm)
Adagio — slow and stately (66–76 bpm)
Andate — at a walking pace (76–108 bpm)
Moderato — moderately (101-110 bpm)
Allegro — fast, quickly and bright (120–139 bpm)
Allegretto — moderately fast (but less so than allegro)
Alla marcia — in the manner of a march
In tempo di valse — in tempo of vals

rallentando — gradual slowing down
a tempo — returns to the base tempo after a ***rallentando***

Articulation

Legato. Notes are played smoothly and connected.

Stacatto. Notes are played separated or detached from its neighbours by a silence.

Fermata (pause)

The note is to be prolonged at the pleasure of the performer.

A la Nanita Nana

Tradicional
Arr: Javier Marcó

Adeste Fideles

John Francis Wade
Arr: Javier Marcó

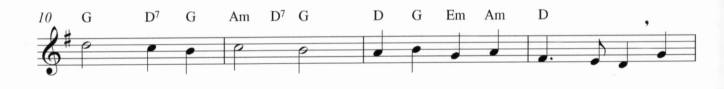

Away in a Manger

James Ramsey Murray
Arr: Javier Marcó

Moderato

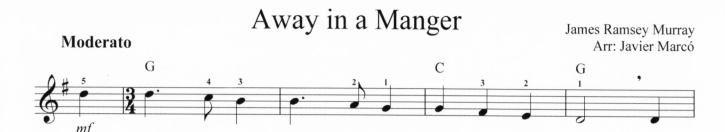

Ça, Bergers, assemblons nous

James Ramsey Murray
Arr: Javier Marcó

Allegro

24

Campana sobre Campana

Tradicional
Arr: Javier Marcó

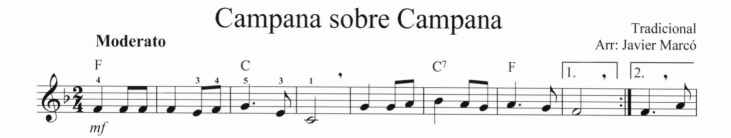

Campanita del Lugar

Tradicional
Arr: Javier Marcó

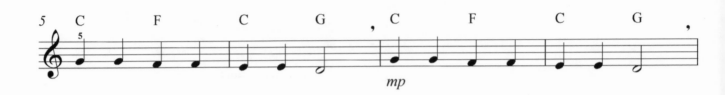

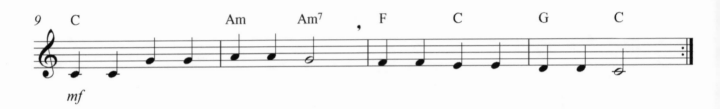

Fröhliche Weihnacht überall

Traditionell
Arr: Javier Marcó

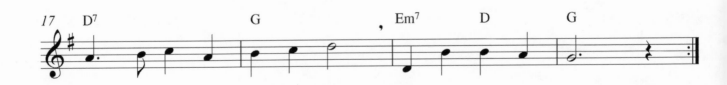

Hark! The Herald Angels Sing

Felix Mendelssohn
Arr. Javier Marcó

Allegro

Il est né, le divin Enfant!

Traditionnel
Arr: Javier Marcó

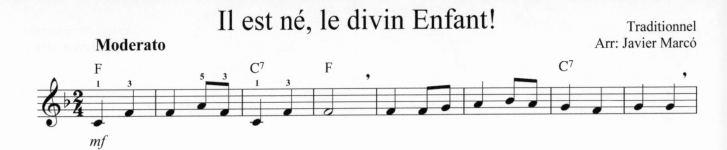

Jingle Bells

James Lord Pierpont
Arr. Javier Marcó

Joy To The World

Georg Friedrich Händel
Arr. Javier Marcó

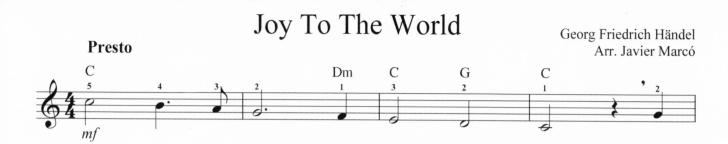

33

La marche des Rois

Georges Bizet
Arr: Javier Marcó

Allegro

Leise rieselt der Schnee

Eduard Ebel
Arr. Javier Marcó

Andante

mf

Les Anges dans nos Campagnes

Traditionnel
Arr: Javier Marcó

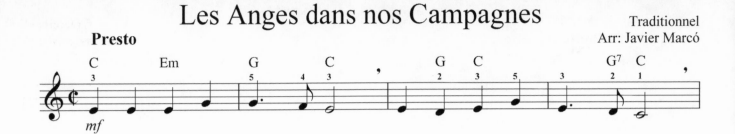

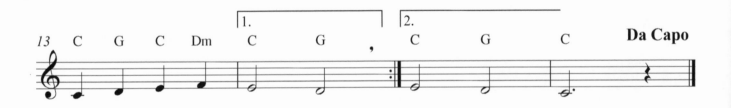

Los Peces en el Río

Tradicional
Arr: Javier Marcó

Moderato

Minuit, chrétiens

Adolphe Adam
Arr: Javier Marcó

BALTHASSAR   MELCHOR   GASPAR

O Tannenbaum

Traditionell
Arr: Javier Marcó

Moderato

Still, Still, Still

Traditionell
Arr: Javier Marcó

Andante

Stille Nacht, heilige Nacht

Franz Xaver Gruber
Arr. Javier Marcó

The First Nowell

Traditional
Arr. Javier Marcó

Moderato

Tu scendi dalle stelle

Alfonso María de Ligorio
Arr: Javier Marcó

We Wish You A Merry Christmas

Traditional
Arr. Javier Marcó

Please visit our website to find more titles of our catalog:
www.MarcoMusica.com

Merry Christmas and a happy New Year!

Made in the USA
San Bernardino, CA
01 December 2014